TEN IRISH POETS

TEN IRISH POETS

– an anthology of poems by

George Buchanan, John Hewitt,

Padraic Fiacc, Pearse Hutchinson,

James Simmons, Michael Hartnett,

Eiléan Ní Chuilleanáin, Michael Foley,

Frank Ormsby & Tom Mathews

edited by

James Simmons

A CARCANET PRESS PUBLICATION

Published with the support of the Arts Council of Northern Ireland and the Arts Council of Eire

SBN 85635 081 8 – cloth
SBN 85635 082 6 – paper

First edition published 1974
by Carcanet Press Limited
266 Councillor Lane
Cheadle Hulme, Cheadle
Cheshire SK8 5PN

Printed in Great Britain by W & J Mackay Limited, Chatham

CONTENTS

9 INTRODUCTION

13 ACKNOWLEDGEMENTS

GEORGE BUCHANAN b. 1904

15 Conversation with Strangers
17 A Wave of Joy
18 War-and-Peace
19 Philanthropy
20 The Animals

JOHN HEWITT b. 1907

21 An Irishman in Coventry
22 Gathering Praties
23 Eager Journey
24 A Victorian Steps Out
24 O Country People
26 Because I Paced My Thought
26 The Scar
27 An Ulster Landowner's Song
28 From the Tibetan

PADRAIC FIACC b. 1924

29 Dirge
29 First Movement
30 The Poet and the Night
30 The Other Man's Wound
31 Alive Alive O
32 Gloss
33 The British Connection
34 The Black and the White
34 Enemies

PEARSE HUTCHINSON b. 1927

36 Connemara
37 Lovers
38 Bright after Dark
38 A Rose and a Book for Sant Jordi
39 Fleadh Cheoil
41 A Man
42 The Nuns at the Medical Lecture

James Simmons b. 1933
44 Ode to Blenheim Square
45 Join Me in Celebrating
45 A Good Thing
46 Husband to Wife
47 Letter to a Jealous Friend
48 Experience
49 Outward Bound
50 Old Gardener
50 Me and the World

Michael Hartnett b. 1941
52 The Person Nox Agonistes
52 The Poet as Black Sheep
53 Crossing the Iron Bridge
54 The Lord Taketh Away
55 The Night before Patricia's Funeral . . .
55 The Third Sonnet
56 A Small Farm
57 The Person as Dreamer
57 All That is Left

Eiléan Ní Chuilleanáin b. 1942
59 Early Recollections
59 Deaths and Engines
60 Evidence
61 The Apparition
62 The Second Voyage
63 A Poem on Change
63 Ferryboat
64 Letter to Pearse Hutchinson
65 Swineherd

Michael Foley b. 1947
66 Recruiting Song
66 Heil Hitler
67 *From* Instead of a Rose
69 The Fall of the Bedsitter King
69 O'Driscoll
71 *From* A la Recherche du Temps Perdu
71 Autumn Leaves
72 I Feel, These Days
73 Into the Breach
74 I'm Scared . . .
75 Sois Sage . . .

Frank Ormsby b. 1947
76 Business as Usual
76 Interim
77 Winter Offerings
78 In Great Victoria Street
79 Floods
79 Dublin Honeymoon
80 Hairy Horseworm
80 Three Domestic Poems
81 Onan
81 McQuade
82 A Brother
82 Castlecoole
82 An Uncle Remembered
83 Virgins

Tom Mathews b. 1945
84 Restless
85 The Singing Lady
86 Anton the Elephant Boy
86 Young Girl's Diary
87 Robert Sat
87 The Cowboy Film
88 Tom's Song
89 Geriatric
89 The Poet with Bad Teeth
89 Foolstop
89 L'Enfant Fatigue
89 Gustav the Great Explorer

91 Notes on Contributors

INTRODUCTION

NATIONALITY preoccupies a people when it is contested. One is not surprised that Yeats and Joyce, in their different ways, were very conscious of being Irish, and the post-rebellion writers like O'Connor felt they had a specifically Irish task to perform. By Beckett's time the sense of nationality is secure enough to be ignored. Northern writers must still be confused in this area whether they are in favour of the political link with Dublin or London. The problem can seem at the same time trivial and inescapable. One can hardly be drawn towards either political set-up very strongly. Any solution that would stop the killing would suit, perhaps; but that sort of feeling can hardly speak with 'passionate intensity'. There is no unjust monster to be endured and resisted; but the uncomfortable knowledge that we and our immediate ancestors have burnt our collective backside, and we must sit on the blister.

I am not sure that there is anything common to these ten poets apart from their being Irish; but that means they have experienced the matter of Ireland first hand, speak or have spoken with an Irish accent, come in contact with Gaelic and read translations. I suspect most of them have read Yeats, Joyce, Synge, Beckett, O'Casey, Kavanagh, MacNeice and Flann O'Brien with peculiar inwardness and intensity. Foley, for instance, hates Yeats with an intensity that is something to do with being an Irishman. Perhaps if they were not Irish I would not be pretty sure of their religious background. I think four were brought up in the Protestant faith and six in the Roman Catholic, although only one or two now belong to a church. Three were brought up in the South and seven in the North. Some have published with Dublin publishers, some in Belfast, some in England. I expect a Dublin writer to be more interested in style and a Belfast writer to be more interested in content, by and large. I suspect there is a more significant distinction to be made between Gaelic-speakers and the rest, not that the former are necessarily influenced by specific forms or writers, but that to have kept up one's Gaelic implies a special attitude to Ireland and her history, and to literature in general.

In fact Pearse Hutchinson writes more plainly and baldly, in certain poems, than any of the Northern and/or non-Gaelic writers (Gaelic is taught in Catholic schools, North and South); but for him it is partly a stylistic exercise in free verse, not just a compulsion to say his say. Buchanan has very obviously got a message, his poems are there to get across his ideas; but the nature and quality of the ideas could not be conveyed without poetry. Whether you call it verse or prose hardly matters.

Scholarly and glossy magazines and finely printed books are more likely to come from Dublin (even Haydn Murphy's *Broadsheet* is a handsome sheet of paper), at their worst, polished coffins: Belfast has always been short of magazines and publishers with literary ambitions: the writers sent their work to London. In 1970 John Montague, John Hewitt, George Buchanan, Seamus Heaney, James Simmons, Derek Mahon, Michael Longley, all Northern poets, were in print with London publishers. Richard Murphy was the only Southern poet I can remember, published there, although Austin Clarke and Thomas Kinsella, published by the Dolmen Press in Dublin, were distributed in England by O.U.P. But then, in the last ten years there seems to have been more poetic activity in the North – not only in this anthology.

These sorts of facts and notions are not of the first importance, but they often exercise us in Ireland. The main thing is to find nourishment in a poet; but other things being equal, if your life is in Ireland then the quality of life in Ireland is more crucial to you than the quality of life elsewhere. Other things are not always equal of course. Tom Mathews writes to me, '*Ten Irish Poets* is a dismal title; this Irish poet objects, especially as he wishes he lived in Newcastle-upon-Tyne and had only to endure the Poulsons of this world. Sweet non-murderous folk, interested in money.' We all look forward to the time when Ireland will be merely corrupt again.

But we cannot wait until that time to attend to the problems we share with the rest of the world. It is not only living in London that makes George Buchanan proclaim the social revolution against aesthetic and emotional impoverishment, emphasising the 'Aphrodisian side'. That was at least part of the platform of the North's great magazine *The Honest Ulsterman*, which came out from County Derry in 1968, at the time of French and American student protest and Civil Rights marches at home. The most hostile reaction to it came from the pulpits; the churches in Ireland are notoriously influential and puritan. I had not come across George Buchanan at the time, and I am particularly excited at the delicacy and warmth with which he presents complex social ideas.

As well as being a good nature poet in the mainstream of English poetry, John Hewitt has spent more literary energy to better purpose on exclusively Ulster problems than any other Irish poet. He does not have a strongly original talent, but you might think of him as the tortoise to W. R. Rodgers's hare: hard work and dedication have rewarded him and his fellow countrymen with a clear mirror to examine their shortcomings and their glories, and a few moments of exalted vision, all the more poignant for being hard won:

> I should have made it plain that I stake my future
> on birds flying in and out of the schoolroom window,

on the council of sunburnt comrades in the sun,
and the picture carried with singing into the temple.

Padraic Fiacc has published comparatively little. I always remember his telling me that though it is many years since he came back from America and settled in Glengormley, local shopkeepers still ask him if he likes it here and if he thinks he'll stay. There is a very personally felt anguish in his passionate, fragmented utterances, apparently set off by the 'bother'. They do not seem to me shaped and connected by a vision or narrative or even a tradition, but their intensity and spare lyricism demanded inclusion.

From Pearse Hutchinson's work I get the impression of a wandering scholar, a wild man and espouser of causes who takes no care for himself . . . and not enough for his work. Much of his published verse is self-indulgent and sentimental but the good poems are very good indeed. It is hard to avoid the word genius, faced with the abundance, feeling, clarity and strength in 'Connemara' and 'Fleadh Cheoil'. There is no pretension or affectation to distort his work when he has something to say and the time to work on it.

Having included some of my own poems from early volumes no longer in print, I had better let others comment on them. P. J. Kavanagh in the *Guardian* spoke of a 'cool, factual tenderness, the like of which I have never seen done better, and seldom seen at all'. Price Turner in *Twentieth Century* wrote, 'Here is an Irish poet capable of anything he sets his mind to.' Everyone seems to enjoy it, but some call it 'slapdash' and 'slick', and Ian Hamilton wrote in the *Observer*, 'Simmons is entertaining in his rather hit-or-miss way.' I think you have to be a clown to play Hamlet these days.

Michael Hartnett is very well thought of in Dublin, and in the North he is the most widely admired Southern poet. He seems to me to have considerable talent and dedication, perhaps a little turned in on himself and obscure. There is certainly a strong ambition to be a poet which is well on the way to being fulfilled.

The only woman in this anthology, Eiléan Ní Chuilleanáin, has a lovely imagination with a sort of hard-boiled magic touch, manifesting on pages the wonder and horror of living:

I want to lie awake at night
Listening to cream crawling to the top of the jug
And the water lying soft in the cistern.

Foley, Ormsby and Mathews were my first and obvious choices when I undertook this book. I have followed their careers from the beginning with interest and often delight. They are very different from each other. Michael Foley is funny about school and scholarship and marriage and his fellow countrymen. He also writes good satirical prose. Detractors say his range is narrow and the texture of his verse thin; but the more I read him the more I see that he does not much repeat himself, that there is real tenderness and proper fierceness, and a subtly original use of the light verse quatrain.

Frank Ormsby has a lot of not so simple humanity and is closest to John Hewitt of all the younger poets. He hangs on to subjects close to his domestic Ulster heart and discovers real discriminations there, and events and scenes. Not apparently gifted with a personal style or mystical insight he justifies hard work and steady application and is rewarded by life yielding up quotidian miracles, and, in the end, originality. Look at his poem on the Belfast Pure Ice & Cold Storage Co. Ltd. ('In Great Victoria Street').

Tom Mathews achieves the seemingly impossible by deriving his style directly from Stevie Smith and yet writing good poems – some coincidence of vision I suppose. His inspiration is not secondary. Perhaps he shows that she was not all that eccentric, and that the angular, almost fey, approach is a way into all sorts of rich common subjects hard to reach by frontal assault.

So, here are ten Irish poets not wanting to draw attention to their nationality or able to deny it.

James Simmons

ACKNOWLEDGEMENTS

For permission to reprint the poems in this anthology, grateful acknowledgement is made to the following:

For George Buchanan: to the author, the Gaberbocchus Press Ltd and Carcanet Press Ltd.
For John Hewitt: to the author and MacGibbon & Kee Ltd.
For Padraic Fiacc: to the author, the Dolmen Press Ltd and the Goldsmith Press.
For Pearse Hutchinson: to the author, the Gallery Press and the Dolmen Press Ltd.
For James Simmons: to the author and the Bodley Head Ltd.
For Michael Hartnett: to the author and the New Writers Press.
For Eiléan Ní Chuilleanáin: to the author and the Gallery Press.
For Michael Foley: to the author and Ulsterman Publications.
For Frank Ormsby: to the author and Ulsterman Publications.
For Tom Mathews: to the author and Ulsterman Publications.

George Buchanan

Conversation with Strangers

Strangers are people we haven't seen before,
the herbage of urban meadows. They're
unexplored countries. A greeting could expose
a fresh geography.

We open the door, go into the blue. The glance of others
is a sunlight. If we don't perceive them
we're without insight or sick. For everyone's invited
to be known: the new knowledge. It may be ignorance
that prevents us from loving our neighbours.

Too facile speaking betrays misery. We're sorry for gabblers
in a public place. We find it hard ourselves
to open our lips, being ponderous from past suffering.

We were reared in privacy, off the street, out of earshot.
'Oh no strangers, please! Only people we know!'

PRIVATE
KEEP OUT

This notice was pinned to the door. Let nobody look over the garden
gate.
They also said: 'Don't refer to this or that in front of the child.' We
became shy,
nervous of the great world. 'Don't speak to strangers' they said.
It seemed starving strangers were waiting to catch at sensual straws,
even
the unsatisfactory bodies of children.

Secrecy was praised. 'Don't visibly enjoy yourself. Find a hotel
apart from the crowd. Swim in a deserted bay. Be careful
what you say on the important subjects: better still, avoid them.
Give copious information on holidays, weather and sport; but hide your
love
and your hate; seem to have a temperature of zero.'

Over against this was J.C.'s message from Palestine
about loving people to whom we haven't been formally introduced.
Easiness with one another would show that the message is heard.
Citizens wouldn't be afraid of making asses of themselves.

Can we de-house and evict ourselves from our solid homes;
a break-out is due. Radio, newspaper
pierce the shell of the house. Ah the relief
as the walls are pierced. Let's be unafraid
if the cameras come, if we're declared open to the public.

Like a girl on the stage who uncovers and states her essence,
we also expose ourselves: our naked fact is our unity.
All inhabitants are joined, even those who don't know it.
Those others are us; they must be hard to despise or kill.
We rear a joint city with a shared construction, hurrying builders, the tink of hammers.
But our ambition can come about only if we imagine our union.

Sneering at the sheer number of others is a drug for self-cultivators
who are also (they won't believe it) particles of the mass.
All of us are; and are filled with that million-made blaze.
Up it comes and burns through us.
As passengers of a train, shoppers, part of an audience,
we notice and are pleased to be with the rest.
Gone the bowing and scraping, the abject public, unworthy to come in.

The broken big-wigs, military heroes, so-called geniuses
are on show like deserted castles: a penny a peep!
The struggle to reclassify ourselves as top men or stars
isn't on. Our study isn't to reach a tower
but go deep like Orpheus into the general world,
to be unguarded with others.

In the park, please, no vilification of many in one place.
If we're world members we can't stiffen as others walk past us,
can't make faces of triumph or fear. Women sit in chairs; a grey-haired lady
shows her legs as one might mention a former wealth;
dandyish young lie under trees. There are bubbles
of affection in the long afternoon. The cold society
we used to know is almost dying. Strangers may cease to be strangers.
We may go to the park as to a room of (near) friends.

A Wave of Joy

1: *rain*
They arrive at the sea, hoping for sun, but the rain is falling,
it will never stop: that's the impression it makes. They enter the hotel.
'So far,' the *Seaside News* reports, 'We've had mist and rain instead
of the sunshine we hoped for.' On the front page

a HOLIDAY DISASTER.

A swing bridge between two cliffs has given way: four visitors will never
go home.
Rain is falling on the esplanade. Persons sit in the hotel, doldrummed,
you might say.
Can we avoid the misery of rain even in a dry house?
Voices of squabbling children give the day a kind of danger, like being
on a steep mountain.

*

2: *sunshine*
Slight difference of light can change a scene.
Today the sun stays out, faces break into smiles.
Parents sit in the garden, a girl
as naked as an allegorical statue is on the seawall.
'Why are you being so absurd?' 'I'm happy.' 'Oh! I suppose that
explains it!'
The children have the future in their hair and cotton shirts: our successors!
But they're insisting on being happy now
as they make a beeline for the pink ice-cream shop.
Entering the water, Susan at seventeen is in that state of balance, the
breasts just right.
Another girl has gentle amused eyes above a wide mouth.
A child calls *Ooh-whoo-hoo*, trying to imitate an unknown bird.
A circle of people on the sand are like a bed of flowers;
they speak with slight undulations.

Next morning an exquisite silence.
Passers stop on the esplanade, struck by the idea
that they may be believing in happiness. They read in the paper:
'From Bergama in Asia Minor it is reported on Tuesday a wave of joy
seemed to pass through the town. Bursts of singing came from the open
windows.

Families ran out into the streets and formed processions . . .' Can that wave
have moved north, touched these shores?
White birds are flying into the cliffs. Has an idea blown in?
Do mermaids come at night and cast a spell?
'Music! Music!' Tourists form a chain and sing. All day on the shore
they're drenched with contentment. As they sing there are tears in Susan's eyes.
'I'm too happy', she says.

*

3: *third phase*
She is weeping among garments scattered on the ground: 'It's no good, it's no good.'
Barking dogs run through the picnic. Drops of rain fall. Eating chocolate
after a cold bathe the medical student explains: 'Very few realise
they're going to die. They've always the classical hope.'
The hatred of later arrivals is obvious.
'What's come over these people, simpering like imbeciles?'
The good time of others is an offence.
'The goings-on! The sand-dunes have become what might be termed a red light district.'

Now it's September. They look at photographs of the summer,
slightly ashamed. Was it the fault of the sun?
Fog comes to the windows. They cannot see, but they hear, cars in the street.
Visibility has been taken from passing noises. The fog throws
each family into itself.
Then the telephone rings. Everywhere the telephones
are ringing. The citizens are trying to find one another.

'Does life have a happy ending?'
'No. But it may have been happy *before* the end.'

War-and-Peace

War is the angry man waving his desperate weapon,
the mushroom cloud in the Pacific Ocean.

Peace is quietude for retired persons sitting on fixed principles, sealed off
from the climate of the contingent in a place where nothing is urgent:
life arranged for academic study, isolated, subdivided, known, a subject
on which X and Y may be taken as the recognized authorities.
It is that evening hymn full of tiredness and repose and low, stop-
worrying voices, the reverend boredom.
It is an eternal luxury cruise in the sun with bingo at night after a heavy
dinner.
Ideal circumstance, the advertised article, expensive ease:
a dream of summoning perfect waiters to the table with a small upward
movement of the eyes.

There is neither war nor peace, there is war-*and*-peace, not either/or but
the two:
rather, if you please, fusion, the play of one into the other, the blend.
War-and-peace isn't either anger or stillness, but persons moving in the
great event of their city every day.
Not peace of mind but the troubled mind:
the warman on the peace path, the peaceman on the war path.
It is the impure joy, the dream and the awakening, the two sides of the
medal:
the anxious holiday, the sunny tour of an Italian lake with a sick girl,
the extravagance of an unhappy time in a delectable but costly place,
friction in the country drawing-room with an outlook of trees,
the senescence and poverty of a great public figure,
the evil politics of a new and exquisitely laid-out town.
It is co-operation with disliked persons, not segregation or party
alignment,
but swallowing resentment, working with detested characters, under-
taking a keen enterprise with untrustworthy associates;
talking of god's love with a bad-tempered clergyman;
drinking a fine claret holding the glass with fingers from which
torturers have drawn the nails;
coming home after dark to a divided family, living in harmony with a
bitch.

Philanthropy

Love of humanity – could it be literal?
The love of which most stand in need is quite simply to be embraced.

Ought sweet self-denying women to be laying themselves out for those
who have no hope that anyone
can any more love them? It is a crying need.
'Ladies bountiful, queens of mercy, souls of charity,
wash, scent yourselves, receive the poor, the emotionally
undernourished.
Send them on their way rejoicing.'

The Animals

The animals are herded slowly from green fields
to be eaten by gentlemen in restaurants. The fish
swim in the river for the pan of an experienced cook.
The wheat grows golden for loaves served at a fair price
in the shops. Even the birds in the trees
are aimed at by happy sportsmen. So the lovers of nature
make fatal advances towards the object of their affection.
And those living in cities who hate the country
and know where their bread-and-butter comes from don't care
as they walk in parks which are innocent of agriculture.

John Hewitt

An Irishman in Coventry

A full year since, I took this eager city,
the tolerance that laced its blatant roar,
its famous steeples and its web of girders,
as image of the state hope argued for,
and scarcely flung a bitter thought behind me
on all that flaws the glory and the grace
which ribbon through the sick, guilt-clotted legend
of my creed-haunted, Godforsaken race.
My rhetoric swung round from steel's high promise
to the precision of the well-gauged tool,
tracing the logic in the vast glass headlands,
the clockwork horse, the comprehensive school.

Then, sudden, by occasion's chance concerted,
in enclave of my nation, but apart,
the jigging dances and the lilting fiddle
stirred the old rage and pity in my heart.
The faces and the voices blurring round me,
the strong hands long familiar with the spade,
the whiskey-tinctured breath, the pious buttons,
called up a people endlessly betrayed
by our own weakness, by the wrongs we suffered
in that long twilight over bog and glen,
by force, by famine and by glittering fables
which gave us martyrs when we needed men,
by faith which had no charity to offer,
by poisoned memory, and by ready wit,
with poverty corroded into malice,
to hit and run and howl when it is hit.

This is our fate: eight hundred years' disaster,
crazily tangled as the Book of Kells:
the dream's distortion and the land's division,
the midnight raiders and the prison cells.
Yet like Lir's children banished to the waters
our hearts still listen for the landward bells.

Gathering Praties

We gathered praties in the upper field
above the road, below the booley mounds,
and the red bracken with its bobbing scuts –
a long four-acre field, half pale with stubble,
half lengthwise ribbed with drills the digger broke
in slow dark showers of mould.

We bent and picked
and flung the tubers, if the proper size,
into the slatted basket, if too small,
into a bucket. When these both were full
we tipped the first into the narrow heaps
to be earthed over later, kind by kind,
Kerr's Pinks and Arran Victors as they came;
the bucket-load was poured into a sack
to serve the feeding for the stock at home.

The strong wind brought its slanted squalls of rain,
some light enough to work through, some too fierce,
which set us running for the low thorn hedge.
Then the half-buried praties daubed with mud
were cold and wet to handle, slithering
from the numb slipping fingers to their place,
till the next drill was scattered clean and dry.

Bend down and pick and fling, each throw a choice;
then the full basket carried to its pit,
and the full bucket tilted in its sack,
till shout of invitation brought us over
to the thorn hedge, and sweet tea from a can
and griddle bread with butter smeared in lumps.

Then raising heavy limbs, relaxed and warm,
into the wind's way and the failing light,
to bend and lift and throw with steady aim
and move through the slow ritual once more.
This till the moon came up, and Pat and Jimmie
began to earth the pits up, which would lie
through the long winter gloom like mounded graves,
narrow and ancient and anonymous.

I left them at the labour and came home,
stiff-jointed, tired, with that slow careful stride
I've learnt already or which lay involved
in some meander of my country blood,
and now runs gracious, happy to be used;
and as I walked, more body than a mind,
my clay-brown fingers felt the weight and pressure
of the round tuber gripped against the palm.
Lord, when we die and our poor minds are bared,
round what strange objects are they clenched and set?

Eager Journey

My mother's father, when he came to die,
summoned his house to join him singing clear
his road to Glory: this, obediently,
they, with schooled voices, did, well versed in praise,
for Methodists were people without fear
of Hell, or doubt of Their Redeemer's Grace.

That first time it was difficult for them
to hold their grief in balanced harmony,
claiming death gate to joy's Jerusalem,
while their brave father struggled with his pain;
but, when the crisis ebbed, relieved to see
the steady breath restored, they wept again.

For days he wrestled, weakening, called for song
when the end beckoned, falling back in sleep
each time God failed to answer. Far too long
and pitiful a vigil for his kin;
a nurse was mustered, so that they might keep
some grip on time, some rhythm of discipline.

One afternoon, slipped down to fetch his tray,
quickly returned, she found him sprawling dead
athwart the tumbled blankets' disarray,
the man who never once had failed a friend,
alone now on that eager journey sped,
not one hosanna trumpeting the end.

A Victorian Steps Out

One summer Sunday in the old Queen's time,
to evening service, for a social mile,
with ribboned bonnet, dolman, muff, umbrella,
leading her adult family with style,
grandmother strode, a straight-backed matriarch:
her retinue reserved, responsible,
nodding where proper courtesy required
as nicely judged as etiquette could spell,
a smile conferred on those whom they knew well.

Then, swinging from behind and catching up,
a band, along the cobbles, pounded by,
with drum and brass and frequent tambourine,
Booth's braided cohort, crimson banners high:
and, after them, the penitential few,
stiff-necked among the roughly jostling crowd,
bullies and blowens from the darkest slums,
raddled with liquor and damnation-proud,
their gestures mocking and their jeering loud.

To the quick consternation of her kin,
my grannie left the pavement, took her place
beside the blessed, tall among the shawls
her ribboned bonnet and her lady's face;
keeping in step the patent-leather boots
with broken boots. Alarmed, her daughters prayed
that none they cared for much should see her now,
gentility's decorum disarrayed,
their hugged pretensions utterly betrayed.

O Country People

O country people, you of the hill farms,
huddled so in darkness I cannot tell
whether the light across the glen is a star,
or the bright lamp spilling over the sill,
I would be neighbourly, would come to terms
with your existence, but you are so far;
there is a wide bog between us, a high wall.

I've tried to learn the smaller parts of speech
in your slow language, but my thoughts need more
flexible shapes to move in, if I am to reach
into the hearth's red heart across the half-door.

You are coarse to my senses, to my washed skin;
I shall maybe learn to wear dung on my heel,
but the slow assurance, the unconscious discipline
informing your vocabulary of skill,
is beyond my mastery, who have followed a trade
three generations now, at counter and desk;
hand me a rake, and I at once, betrayed,
will shed more sweat than is needed for the task.

If I could gear my mind to the year's round,
take season into season without a break,
instead of feeling my heart bound and rebound
because of the full moon or the first snowflake,
I should have gained something. Your secret is pace.
Already in your company I can keep step,
but alone, involved in a headlong race,
I never know the moment when to stop.

I know the level you accept me on,
like a strange bird observed about the house,
or sometimes seen out flying on the moss
that may tomorrow, or next week, be gone,
liable to return without warning
on a May afternoon and away in the morning.

But we are no part of your world, your way,
as a field or a tree is, or a spring well.
We are not held to you by the mesh of kin;
we must always take a step back to begin,
and there are many things you never tell
because we would not know the things you say.

I recognize the limits I can stretch;
even a lifetime among you should leave me strange,
for I could not change enough, and you will not change;
there'd still be levels neither'd ever reach.

And so I cannot ever hope to become,
for all my goodwill toward you, yours to me,
even a phrase or a story which will come
pat to the tongue, part of the tapestry
of apt response, at the appropriate time,
like a wise saw, a joke, an ancient rime
used when the last stack's topped at the day's end,
or when the last lint's carted round the bend.

Because I Paced My Thought

Because I paced my thought by the natural world,
the earth organic, renewed with the palpable seasons,
rather than the city falling ruinous, slowly
by weather and use, swiftly by bomb and argument,

I found myself alone who had hoped for attention.
If one listened a moment he murmured his dissent:
this is an idle game for a cowardly mind.
The day is urgent. The sun is not on the agenda.

And some who hated the city and man's unreasoning acts
remarked: He is no ally. He does not say that
Power and Hate are the engines of human treason.
There is no answering love in the yellowing leaf.

I should have made it plain that I stake my future
on birds flying in and out of the schoolroom-window,
on the council of sunburnt comrades in the sun,
and the picture carried with singing into the temple.

The Scar

There's not a chance now that I might recover
one syllable of what that sick man said,
tapping upon my great-grandmother's shutter,
and begging, I was told, a piece of bread,
for on his tainted breath there hung infection
rank from the cabins of the stricken west,

the spores from black potato-stalks, the spittle
mottled with poison in his rattling chest;
and she, who, by her nature, quickly answered,
accepted in return the famine-fever;
and that chance meeting, that brief confrontation,
conscribed me of the Irishry for ever.

Though much I cherish is outside their vision,
and much they prize I have no claim to share,
yet in that woman's death I found my nation:
the old wound aches and shows its fellow-scar.

An Ulster Landowner's Song

I'm Major This or Captain That,
MC and DSO.
This Orange Lily in my hat
I sometimes wear for show,

so long as I can walk my dogs
around the old estate,
and keep the Fenians in their bogs,
and peasants at the gate.

I meet my tenants, decent men,
in Lodge or market day,
and all seems safe till, now and then,
they start a small affray.

They stirred up an unwelcome noise,
it set my nerves on edge,
that day they beat those girls and boys
across Burntollet Bridge,

with journalists and cameras there
to send in their reports.
The world no longer seems to care
for healthy country sports.

From the Tibetan

In my native province when I was young
the lamas were presumed to be dishonest,
not because they were more wicked than the rest
but their calling gave them more scope.

They were not expected to be philosophers
or poets, for they were not educated persons;
theories were as inconceivable as books
in their satchels. All they were asked
was to provide certain familiar noises
on fixed occasions of the calendar,
spinning the wheels with ritual fervour
and chanting of *The Emperor's Tunic*
and *The Great Wall of China*.

For the rest of their time it was anticipated
that they should work hard rewarding their families,
promoting their nephews, replenishing their stores,
and accepting presents from contractors.
Traditionally, all this was to be done with a show
of cordiality, with handclasps, salutes,
conspicuous finger-signals and audible passwords:
the effect which it was desired to produce
being that of reluctant necessity
for complicated manoeuvre.

Now I am older and live in the suburbs of the capital,
I find that the lamas here are very much the same,
save that the rewarding, promoting, replenishing is
done on their behalf by a permanent secretariat,
leaving them more time to devote to the illusion
of exercising power; this forces them to acquire
a more sophisticated vocabulary; indeed,
one or two of them have written books:
In my native province this
would have been looked upon with disfavour,
for we are a simple people.

Padraic Fiacc

Dirge

Against the down twilighting
I came on my gold bee's
Fur-sheen burnt black
Gold gone rust between
Bars where wings once were
On the little fellow's back.

I made this shelter for
Creatures to be in
Drinking honey and planting
Sea-green clover.
Who killed my brazen pet
Every bold flower's boy-lover?

Ancient sages would find
This a danger sign
A plague's beginning
Would take cover
Down under the earth and
Drown themselves in wine!

First Movement

Low clouds yellow in a mist wind
Sift on far-off ards
Drift hazily . . .

I was born on such a morning
Smelling of the Bone Yards

The smoking chimneys over
                    the slate roof-tops
The wayward storm birds

And to the east where morning is
the sea
And to the west where evening is
the sea
Threatening with danger
and it
Would always darken suddenly.

The Poet and the Night

Sleet wind rattles the telegraph
Wires in winter to spring wet.

Debussy, if dying, is not dead yet
Gives himself and us a cloud-bath!

The poet, trying to, does forget
On land, the bombs, at sea, the mines

And in his own body

Cancer of the intestines.

The Other Man's Wound

for James Simmons

I
In the communal shower, after the drowning
We felt like Jews in Nazi Germany:

The water, flagellating down, took on
Something of the hostility in that
dooms
– day for all who are born . . .

Soaping our sweat to goose pimples, we
Kept thinking about us, not him.

II
A fly hanging upside down
Come in to die, my friend

Climbing the government-forbidden
Mountain hill-wall
                                        fell
Thirty to fifty feet,
                                        has
A hole in his right arm
And something tin

Rattles the bittern-cock's boom
Through his teeth as in sex.

'Did you hurt yourself?' I said

And he said 'Did you?'

Alive Alive O

The altar boy from a Mass for the dead
Romps through the streets of the town

Lolls on brick studded grass
Jumps up, bolts back down

With wild pup eyes . . .

This morning at twist of winter to
                                                            spring
Small hands clutched a big brass cross
Followed the stern brow of the priest

Encircle the man in the box . . .

A bell-tossed head sneezed
In a blue daze of incense on

Shrivelled bit lips, then
Just to stay awake, prayed

Too loud for the man to be at rest . . .

O now where has he got to
But climbed an apple tree!

Gloss

Nor truth nor good did they know
But beauty burning away.

They were the dark earth people
of old
Restive in the clay . . .

Deirdre watched Naisi die
And great King Conor of himself
said

'Did you ever see a bottomless
bucket
In the muck discarded?'

And comradely Dermot was destroyed by Fionn

Because of the beauty of a girl.

Because of the beauty of a girl
The sky went raging on fire

And the sea was pushed out into
rage.

They were the dark earth people
of old

And Deirdre pitched herself into
the sea.

Turn the page. Turn the page.

The British Connection

In Belfast, Europe, your man
Met the Military come to raid
The house:
               'Over my dead body
Sir,' he said, brandishing
A real-life sword from some
Old half forgotten war . . .

And youths with real bows and arrows
And coppers and marbles good as bullets
And old time thrupenny bits and stones
Screws, bolts, nuts, (Belfast confetti)

And kitchen knives, pokers, Guinness tins
And nail-bombs down by the Shore Road

And guns under the harbour wharf
And bullets in the docker's tea tin
And gelignite in the tool shed
And grenades in the pantry larder
And weed killer and sugar
And acid in the french letter

And sodium chloride and nitrates
In the suburban garage
In the boot of the car

And guns in the oven grill
And guns in the spinster's shift

And ammunition and more more
Guns in the broken down rusted
Merry-Go-Round in the Scrap Yard

Almost as many hard-on
Guns as there are union jacks.

The Black and the White

Sinking on iron streets, the bin-lid
-shielded, battleship-grey-faced kids

Shinny up the lamp post, cannot tear
Themselves away, refuse to come in

From the dying lost day they douse
With petrol and set the town's holy

Cows on fire, as if the burning bus
or car
Could light up their eyes ever, much
less
The burning of our own kitchen houses

Coming over the TV screen had held
Any surprises, for really, we wallow
in this old

Time western where the 'savages' are
bad
And lost the war because
the white men
Always have to be the Good Guys.

Enemies

I
Belfast makes a tall boy
Bonfire for bonfirenight

To burn in effigy the guy
Calls himself a fellow Christ-

ian! The gall of this guy, we
Burn instead of crucify

Christ, the enemy . . .

II
At the Gas and Electric Offices
Black boats with white sails
Float down the stairs

Frightening the five year old
wee Protestant girls . . .

'Nuns, nuns,' one of them yells
'When are yez go'n' to git
morried?'

Pearse Hutchinson

Connemara

for Luis Cardoza y Aragón

Much good may it do me to steal prayers from Isaac
of Nineveh; much good to recall one drunken summer
afternoon when a greengage-tree glowed like God;
much good, an infinitesimal white fish-bone
prised from my throat and gleaming in the penumbra
of a doctor's room and whiter
than any whiteness while the traffic roared,
the pulsing unbearable decibels of July sun,
outside the ajar shutters – for what does all that prayer
come down to now but mere fear.
I stand, Cois Fharraige, watching
two swans and four geese on grey water
under a grey sky, lichen black or mustard
on grey and rust-coloured rocks, by the road-side
a knee-high yellow pole with a red band at the top
luminous at night: there must be a prayer here
but all I can catch is fear: I pray, quite panic-stricken,
to God to keep my ageing, weakened bowels closed
until we reach a hotel, I writhe in ludicrosity, beseech
the cough not rack. Still fear, and worse than ever.
(The fear of decaying food in a widowed bachelor kitchen.)
I pray against barbed wire.

In kelp cormorant fuchsia foxglove country,
collies and black-faced cream-wooled sheep,
drystone walls at once darker and brighter after the rain,
the quartz gleaming whiter in the gloaming,
I name Ben Gorm, Blue Peak, tingling day-luminous blue
in the distance, green close-to at Leenaun, I name
Lough Doo, Black Lake, Málaga-blue in the distance, harsh
blackish near-to. There must be prayers here,
I whinge against the barbed wire
of disablement, panic.

Seborrhea, cellulitis, rumplefyke.
Amylozene, Grunovit, Kaopectate.

I throw a dandelion down into the green-brown
stream of a nameless waterfall,
I watch – the right, lovely sound for a lovely meaning –
the yellow flower swirl aside out of the current,
amid mild suds be calm.
I pluck and throw
a second one down, it drifts under the bridge
back towards the fall. Hirpling to the other side
I crane over, peer; the flower does not appear.
Am I praying? Offering? Perhaps I'm praying
a true prayer.

Under the conical menace of a Gothic mountain,
in these green fields I pray against barbed wire,
and never forget to take my pills.

Lovers

You with full hands
keep them closed, like fists;
use the warm wealth you clutch in there
only for loading blows;
a hundred birds in a cage on the latch:
none of the birds can fly.
But at times you forget, relax,
the knuckles unwhiten,
a grain of warmth slips out between fingers.
Feathers move gently.

While I advance vainly, blowing my top,
professionally proffering my open
wide wide open palms,
for all comers to lick.
Splayed. Eager. Empty.
Not even a tearlet of sweat.
Would-be generous, poor.

Bright after Dark

for Sebastian Ryan

In the first country,
what you must do when the cow stops giving milk
is climb, after dark, a certain hill,
and play the flute: to kill your scheming neighbour's curse.
If you can find a silver flute to play,
the spell will break all the faster, the surer.
But silver is not essential. But: the job must
be done after dark:
otherwise, it won't work.

In the second country,
when you send a child out of the house at night,
after dark, you must, if you wish it well,
take, from the fire, a burnt-out cinder
and place it on the palm of the child's hand
to guard the child against the dangers of the dark.
The cinder, in this good function, is called aingeal,
meaning angel.

In the third country,
if you take a journey at night, above all
in the blind night of ebony, so good for witches to work in,
you dare not rely on fireflies for light,
for theirs is a brief, inconstant glow. What you must hope
is that someone before you has dropped grains of maize
on the ground to light your way; and you must drop
grains of maize for whoever comes after you:
for only maize can light the way on a dark night.

A Rose and a Book for Sant Jordi

Brave Galinsoga strode up the aisle,
pocket tyrant of a half-cowed country,
the only beautiful thing about him his name,
and called, as the people were singing to God in their own language,
what they were singing in
shit. Proud Galinsoga, the boss-man's countryman,

the overpaid hireling, the white-collar jackboot-in-office,
called the word loud and clear, over and again,
just as the people were learning, at last, again,
the almost-forgotten, almost-undreamt-of feeling of freedom to sing
to God in their own language.
He got as far as the altar-rails, and then they seized him and threw him
out.

Next day both to his private mailbox and his editorial office
there came an avalanche of little gift-packets
neatly tied in pink or yellow ribbons
containing small turds,
it being the national day, the day of Sant Jordi,
and the custom having been and beginning to be again, a bit,
to sing to God in their own language,
on that day, their day.

Galinsoga: beautiful nine-letter name.

Fleadh Cheoil

Subtle capering on a simple thought,
the vindicated music soaring out
each other door in a mean twisting main street,
flute-player, fiddler and penny-whistler
concentrating on one sense only
such a wild elegance of energy gay and sad
few clouds of lust or vanity could form;
the mind kept cool, the heart kept warm;
therein the miracle, three days and nights
so many dances played and so much drinking done,
so many voices raised in singing but none
in anger nor any fist in harm –
Saint Patrick's Day in Cambridge Circus might
have been some other nation's trough of shame.

Hotel-back-room, pub-snug, and large open lounges
made the mean street like a Latin fête,
music for once taking all harm out –
from even the bunting's pathetic blunderings,
and the many mean publicans making money fast,
hand over fat fist, pouring the flat

western porter from black-chipped white enamel,
Dervorgilla's penitent chapel
crumbling arch archaic but east,
only music now releasing her people
like Sweeney's cousins on a branch unable
to find his words, but using music
for all articulateness.

But still the shabby county-town was full,
en fête; on fire with peace – for all
the black-and-white contortionists bred
from black-and-white married ever said.
From Easter Snow and Scartaglin
the men with nimble fingers came
in dowdy Sunday suits,
from Kirkintilloch and Ladbroke Grove came back
in flashy ties and frumpish hats,
to play an ancient music, make it new.
A stranger manner of telling than words can do,
a strange manner, both less and more than words or Bach,
but like, that Whitsuntide, stained-glass in summer,
high noon, rose window, Benedictbeuern pleasure,
and Seán O Neachtain's loving singing wood,
an Nollaig sa tSamhradh.

Owls and eagles, clerks and navvies,
ex-British Tommies in drab civvies,
and glorious-patriots whose wild black brindled hair
stood up for the trench-coats they had no need to wear
that tranquil carnival weekend,
when all the boastful maladies got cured –
the faction-fighting magniloquence,
devoid of charity or amorous sense,
the sun-shunning pubs, the trips to Knock.

One said to me: 'There's heart in that',
pointing at: a thick-set man of middle age,
a thick red drinker's face,
and eyes as bright as good stained-glass,
who played on and on and on
a cheap tin-whistle, as if no race

for petty honours had ever come to pass
on earth, or his race to a stale pass;
tapping one black boot on a white flag,
and us crowding, craning, in at the door,
gaining, and storing up, the heart in that.
With him a boy about eighteen,
tall and thin, but, easy to be seen,
Clare still written all over him
despite his eighteen months among the trim
scaffoldings and grim digs of England;
resting his own tin-whistle for his mentor's riff,
pushing back, with a big red hand, the dank mousy quiff,
turning to me to say, 'You know what I think of it,
over there?
Over there, you're free.'
Repeating the word 'free', as gay and sad as his music,
repeating the word, the large bright eyes convinced
of what the red mouth said, convinced beyond
shaming or furtiveness, a thousand preachers,
mothers and leader-writers wasting their breath
on the sweet, foggy, distant-city air.
Then he went on playing as if there never were
either a famed injustice or a parish glare.

Ennis.

An Nollaig sa tSamhradh: Christmas in Summer. From a love-song by Seán O Neachtain, Roscommon-born poet and novelist (1655–1728).

A Man

A man is screaming in his bathroom,
and the neighbours mistake it for singing.
The door is locked, the windows barred,
but the noise goes through the walls,
and the neighbours mistake it for singing.
One says: 'He hasn't a note in his head,'
another: 'He sounds happy, the monster,'
and a foreigner strolling in the street below
marvels: 'What exuberance, what brio
these people have!'

What noise
can the man himself think he is making?

The Nuns at the Medical Lecture

The nuns at the medical lecture have rose faces
like babies surprised into wisdom, the clerical students
passing the pub look slightly scared, but mainly
serene, the cultured ancient cod in his lamplit room
lined with the desert fathers and the village idiots
and the palace pornographs, warms the port in his palm
and remarks that passion rages most after innocence
because it is innocent, and rages to corrupt;
the young spongers gape, consoling themselves
for the gap between drinks by considering sagacity,
we all sometimes talk like a tenth-rate
so understanding confessor.

Always the maligned force that carries light
achieves its kind revenge, and the velveteen shield
of every proud prig erupts in termed lunacy;
the man in dark glasses was, fancy, at the very same
college a vague few years ago, and buys the boy
a pint; the foreign landlady sends in coffee
at odd hours and doesn't charge it;
the brilliant friend suddenly weeps, and pity
does the trick; the adolescent skeleton
marionettes in front of the glistening wardrobe;
the nun fingertips her scraped pate with pride,
and the masseur, the barber, the preacher, and the prior . . .

So like whiskey creates anger, and love creates greed,
as the lizard creates the sun, and the bull sand,
we have created your sin, we conceived
the death of your innocence.
With all our ageing need, we have corrupted you,
as the air corrupts the bud into flower,
as the fountain corrupts the air.

Let us go, and you in front with sackcloth and ashes
over silk, and lament the beautiful ivory death
all would have walked through had we not met –
in a carnival of personal pronouns, a battle of flowers
and roots, wear this laughter to shreds.

James Simmons

Ode to Blenheim Square

for George Campbell

Declining houses, still tall,
On two sides of the square,
On two sides a crumbling wall,
Enclose a garden, worn bare
Of grass in bald patches, defaced
By rubbish. The railings and gate,
Removed for the last war, were not replaced,
And now it is too late;
The people that this square was built to please
Have long since gone,
And artists, students, refugees,
Once admitted, cling on.

Even the trees are dirty to touch,
The undug clay, hard:
A bit of Nature, but not much
Better than a concrete yard.
You can't lie down for dog-shit.
But every morning, lovely, lonely,
Through white mist, lit
By the hidden sun, only
Greenness and brightness show,
And, sharp against the sky, aloof,
As your eyes reach from below,
The everywhere elegant lines of branch and roof.
The blemishes don't show
At sunset either,
Or under snow.
That beauty is hidden is in its favour;
I don't give garden parties.
I am content
To have no better times than these,
And no other environment.

Last Sunday I came
Downstairs and saw the door, ajar,
And grimed fanlight frame
The garden,
While I stood inside:
The Dutch painters' view in reverse
Also in my house-pride
Being perverse.
But a cheap rent on what I love
Is guaranteed by decay:
Rich and poor disapprove
In the same way.

Join Me in Celebrating

Join me in celebrating
This unhoped for gift
She has brought me sweating
In a crumpled shift.
Pushed through my wife,
My letter-box, appears
A present of life,
Bald head and flattened ears,
Parcelled in blood and slime,
A loosely wrapped thing,
Unlabelled but on time,
String dangling.
I wouldn't change my condition
For freedom, cash, applause,
Rebirth of young ambition
Or faith in Santa Claus.

A Good Thing

Too many colleagues smile at me
whom I have hardly seen,
and some who wish me little good.
What the hell do they mean?

To say, 'I love you', is like a smile,
neither false nor true.
To see exactly what I mean,
watch me, see what I do.

At a drunken party months ago
I shared an easy chair
with this girl and unzipped her dress
and laid her whole back bare,

and felt the common magic
that fingers feel on skin,
and felt my lips on her cool lips,
and her little tongue come in.

One hand un-clipped her bra
another gently cupped a breast,
and then, for lack of energy,
we joined the rest.

More privacy and energy
confirmed that happy start,
but if she married or left town
it wouldn't break my heart.

Such girls are like the sunshine,
good food and bitter beer.
I smile at you and say, 'I love you',
Is my meaning clear?

Husband to Wife

When I consider how your life was spent
before we met, I see a parked car
where some man took you, dear, with your consent
and helped to make you what you are.
From both of you there is the smell of beer,
I feel you thrilled at last to be alone,
not missing me – well, how could I be here! –
exploring him and being explored and known.

My fancy pushes towards pornography
the necessary sweet acts of lust.
Then you undid his fly, unblushingly,
with cool hands, then a joke, a smile of trust,
then took his weight and smelt and felt his breath,
then held and guided underneath your skin
his rosy, swelling penis in a sheath,
filling you up as it came in,

just as mine does, my bride.
Just as mine does. Such thoughts have made me sweat
and wrestle, hours, no, years, against my pride.
And, to be honest, I am wrestling yet.

You are because you were, and when I love
I love because and not in spite of this,
and you, not waiting till I rise above
my past, must cleave to my uneasiness.

Letter to a Jealous Friend

You could not say, 'What now?' you said, 'Too late!'
What energies bad principles have spilt.
Old friend, you hate me and you aggravate
Me, for I will not feel regret or guilt

When your white face stares at me from the door
With wizard eyes that change the three of us
Into a cuckold, a roué, a whore –
A stupid, ugly metamorphosis.

Acquaintances are mocking my belief
That we could still be friends when it was known.
I tremble when you treat me like a thief;
But I touched nothing you can call your own.

A child might own the doll it sleeps beside
And men own money and what money buys;
But no one earns a friend or owns his bride
However much he needs or hard he tries.

You try to run me over with your bus
And call me out of restaurants to fight.
I smile weakly and wait for all the fuss
To fade. I need to get my sleep at night.

I hear in some domestic tiff she tossed
Our love at you and scored. Each time I try
To fit that in my creed I lose my place.
There's more in animals than meets the eye.

Sweet fun and freedom didn't last for long
With you out shouting we'd betrayed your trust.
We said it was our business. We were wrong.
Your jealousy's as natural as our lust.

Our thoughts of other people paralyse
Our minds and make us act the silly parts
We think they cast us in. Feeling their eyes
On us, we seem to lose touch with our hearts.

Crippled by hate you have to crouch in dude
Levis and dark glasses, glaring at us.
We have to lie unnaturally nude
And vulnerable, trapped, ridiculous.

Experience

'I want to fight you,' he said in a Belfast accent.
Amazed and scared, with hurried words I resisted.
'Fighting solves nothing. Tell me how I've annoyed you,'
I said. But more insulted the man persisted.

In the lavatory he squared his fists and approached me:
'Now you can talk.' I backed over cold stone in
A room that contained us and joined us. 'It's all so silly,'
I pleaded, searching for spaces to be alone in.

I shrank from his strangeness, not only afraid.
But at last of course I suffered what could not be delayed,

The innocuous struggle, the fighting words, 'bastard' and 'fuck',
A torn shirt and my lip numb and bloody,
My anger and – strange – the feel of my own body
New to me, as I struck, as he struck.

Outward Bound

Two campers (King Lear and his clown?)
smile to see the skies come down.
The shaken mind finds metaphors
in winds that shake the great outdoors.
As roofs and fences fall in storms
the tranquil mind's protective forms
collapse when passion, grief and fear,
stir. We shall spend a fortnight here.

To this small wilderness we bring
ourselves to play at suffering,
to swim in lonely bays, immerse
in the destructive elements, nurse
our bare forked bodies by wood fires
where Ox-tail soup in mugs inspires
the tender flesh. By rocks we cough
and shiver in the wind, throw off
what history has lent, and lie
naked, alone, under the sky.

Of course not one of us prefers
the cold, we are sun-worshippers,
wilderness and storm defiers,
neither masochists nor liars.

Cheeks whipped by freezing rain go numb,
the baffled blood is stirred, will come
again, glowing, like my mind when Lear
speaks in the words of Shakespeare.
Under duress trying to sing
in tune, foretasting suffering
that we will swallow whole. The storm
endured, we hope to come to harm

at home, with better dignity
or style or courage. Anyway
I like to camp and read *King Lear*.
We had a lovely fortnight here.

Old Gardener

I kneel down painfully and touch the dirty lace
Of cabbage leaves, all crinkled like my face
And preying hands, twisted, but still able
To pluck out weeds between the vegetables
And give them space freely to suck and chew
The soil their muscular stalks stick through.

Fifty years I've filled boxes for market
For men to buy and eat, digest and defecate.
The roar of teeth clashing fills my inner
Ear. The world is always at dinner.
I hear the jaws of caterpillars ravage
The thick leaves of the hungry cabbage.

Older, weaker, never to be fatter,
I am frightened of chewing, chewing, chewing. Matter
Is eating matter, and I, who buy and sell
And nurture ravagers, am chewed as well,
Living between Jehovah's jaws until
The garden is empty and his grinders are still.

Me and the World

I live with photographs
For the world, my girl, is away mostly,
Estranged by flaws of mine or withdrawn
For her own reasons. She will always surprise me,
And some days when I open my eyes
She is present to every sense.
It makes all the difference.
My hands answer faster than blind men
At braille, learn by the lover's touch
What news I need in all her Double Dutch:

And ears and eyes are distinct and expert by sorrow
Knowing she is here today and gone tomorrow.

Fidgeting bird song, the tram's lurch and slide
Are henceforward my girl's perfect nonsense.
Together we walk, in the bar she sits at my side.
Her pencil stump worn down with words,
My left hand, resting face down on her table,
Her amber pint of beer, tobacco shreds,
This atmosphere of this, her morning,
Are on speaking terms with my head.
Outside the crippled houses respond
To the continual miracle of sun and dust.
Roofs, railings and the time of year
Walk beautifully together because they must.
And rare colours, blended by hard wear,
On cheap cottons of city children
Invite, not pity, but the satisfaction of love.
The rare ointment of formal praise
Is suddenly useful on such wedding days.

I serve and sway the land. Standing
More like a child than lover, I hold her hand
And listen. Missing perhaps the point of the story,
Grateful, stupid, smiling, I share the glory.

My smile is genuine, though when she laughs
I don't forget my jar to warm the bed, my photographs.

Michael Hartnett

The Person Nox Agonistes

Every rural cage has prisoners,
every small hill-sheltered townland,
every whitewashed tourist'd village
holds a heart that cannot speak out,
lives a life of angered murmurs.
Over eleven pints of Guinness,
over fifty bitter Woodbines,
we have talked about our futures:
we have found no quick solution.

If one is lax in adoration,
still the priests have satisfaction
by our appearance every Sunday.
If to small tyrant employers
we bring the benefit of Unions
we are unemployed eccentrics.

If what we love is all corruption,
we must sacrifice our reason,
we must sit here in this townland
talking always of the future,
finding out no quick solutions,
over eleven pints of Guinness,
over fifty bitter Woodbines.

The Poet as Black Sheep

I have seen him dine
in middle-class surroundings
his manners refined,
as his family around him
talk about nothing,
one of their favourite theses.

I have seen him lying
between the street and pavement,

atoning, dying
for their sins: the fittest payment
he can make for them:
to get drunk and go to pieces.

On his father's face
in sparse lines etched out by ice,
the puritan race
has come to its zenith of grey spite,
its climax of hate,
its essence of frigidity.

Let the bourgeoise beware,
who could not control this head
and kept it in their care
until the brain bled:
this head is a poet's head,
this head holds a galaxy.

Crossing the Iron Bridge

'My dear brethren, boys and girls, today is a glorious day! Here we have a hundred lambs of our flock, the cream of the town, about to receive the Body and Blood of Christ, about to become Children of God, and to enter into a miraculous Union with Jesus . . .'

Into the cobweb-coloured light,
by arms in white rosettes,
I walked up Maiden Street
across the Iron Bridge
to seek my Christ.

'It will be a wonderful moment when the very Body and Blood of Our Lord Jesus Christ is placed upon your tongues – what joy there will be in Heaven! So many valuable little souls safely into the Fold! Look behind the Altar! There will be angels there, ascending and descending, singing songs of joy . . .'

Into the incense-coloured light,
my arms in white rosettes,
I walked the marbled floor
apast parental eyes
to seek my Christ.

'Christ will be standing there in all His Glory, his Virgin Mother will smile and there will be a great singing in Heaven . . .'

Under the gilded candle-light,
my arms in white rosettes,
my mouth enclosed my God,
I waited at the rail
to find my Christ.

'There will be the glow of God in your veins, your souls will be at one with Heaven: if you were to die today, angels would open the Gates of Paradise, and with great rejoicing bear you in . . .'

Back to the human-hampered light,
my arms in white rosettes,
I walked: my faith was dead.
Instead of glory on my tongue
there was the taste of bread.

The Lord Taketh Away

In virgin cloisters from fourteen
It was taught as the only life:
Before the body made its moves
The best wife was the spiritual wife.

They preached the convent was the bar
Between the wanted and the wild
And poured their holy lies upon
The immaculate logic of this child.

For her I wrote impotent songs,
Transparent and slight as tears,
And offered her mortal happiness
For some unspecified years.

Because for her death was
The consequence of a kiss,
While Christ, as ghostly husband,
Offered immortal bliss.

I fought, that devious lessons
Might somehow be undone,
But the odds were three to one:
Father and Son and Holy Ghost.
I had no chance against such a host.

The Night before Patricia's Funeral . . .

the night before Patricia's funeral in 1951,
I stayed up late talking to my father.

how goes the night, boy?
    the moon is down:
    dark is the town
    in this nightfall.
how goes the night, boy?
    soon is her funeral,
    her small white burial.
she was my threeyears child,
her honey hair, her eyes
small ovals of thrush-eggs.
how goes the night, boy?
    it is late: lace
    at the window
    blows back in the wind.
how goes the night, boy?
    – Oh, my poor white fawn!
how goes the night, boy?
    it is dawn.

The Third Sonnet

Here be the burnings, all for wizardry,
Done by the Bishop of Würzburg city:

The steward of the Senate, named Gering,
Senator Baunach, fattest man in town,
And Goebel's child, a girl most beautiful:
Silberhans, a minstrel awandering,

And a blind girl whose skin was very brown,
And a student, new from the Music School.

Liebler's daughter: Madame Knertz: Schwartz a priest –
Nor was the innkeeper of Klingen released.
Valkenberger's little daughter, at home
Was executed, burnt outside her door:

Also some travellers going to Rome,
And Ehling a vicar, and many more.

A Small Farm

All the perversions of the soul
I learnt on a small farm.
How to do the neighbours harm
by magic, how to hate.
I was abandoned to their tragedies,
minor but unhealing:
bitterness over boggy land,
casual stealing of crops,
venomous cardgames
across swearing tables,
a little music on the road,
a little peace in decrepit stables.
Here were rosarybeads,
a bleeding face,
the glinting doors
that did encase
their cutler needs,
their plates, their knives,
the cracked calendars
of their lives.

I was abandoned to their tragedies
and began to count the birds,
to deduct secrets in the kitchen cold
and to avoid among my nameless weeds
the civil war of that household.

The Person as Dreamer: We Talk about the Future

. . . it has to be a hill,
high, of course, and twilit.
There have to be some birds,
all sadly audible:
a necessary haze,
and small wristlets of rain:
yes, and a tremendous
air of satisfaction.
Both of us shall be old
and both our wives, of course,
have died, young, and tragic.
And all our children have
gone their far ways, estranged,
or else not begotten.
We have been through a war,
been hungry, and heroes:
and here we are now, calm,
fed, and reminiscent.
The hills are old, silent:
our pipe-smoke rises up.
We have come a long way . . .

All That is Left . . .

All that is left and definite
is the skull:
the dull fibres and flesh are gone.
the long femur survives perhaps,
or the wreck of ribs,
but nothing plasmic.
no alien could figure how it loved,
longed to avoid death.
he could perhaps by reconstruction
see it stood,
see, if the tarsals were intact,
it fled, it grasped.
but how could sight be guessed at,
the eyeballs gone?

how could envision blood,
arteries and heart
flaked down and dusted?
or hair, wave-long and starred,
that sparked out under fingers,
under amber?
all that is left and definite
is the skull full of cockroaches,
and hollow fragile strands in twos
rayed like tendrils
out about a root.

Eiléan Ní Chuilleanáin

Early Recollections

If I produce paralysis in verse
Where anger would be more suitable,
Could it be because my education
Left out the sight of death?
They never waked my aunt Nora in the front parlour;
Our cats hunted mice but never
Showed us what they killed.
I was born in the war but never noticed.
My aunt Nora is still in the best of health
And her best china has not been changed or broken.
Dust has not settled on it; I noticed it first
The same year that I saw
How the colours of stones change as water
Dries off them after rain.
I know how things begin to happen
But never expect an end.

Dearest,
            if I can never write 'goodbye'
On the torn final sheet, do not
Investigate my adult life but try
Where I started. My
Childhood gave me hope
And no warnings.
I discovered the habits of moss
That secretly freezes the stone,
Rust softly biting the hinges
To keep the door always open.
I became aware of truth
Like the tide helplessly rising and falling in one place.

Deaths and Engines

We came down above the houses
In a stiff curve, and
At the edge of Paris airport

Saw an empty tunnel
– The back half of a plane, black
On the snow, nobody near it,
Tubular, burnt-out and frozen.

When we faced again
The snow-white runways in the dark
No sound came over
The loudspeakers, except the sighs
Of the lonely pilot.

The cold of metal wings is contagious:
Soon you will need wings of your own,
Cornered in the angle where
Time and life like a knife and fork
Cross, and the lifeline in your palm
Breaks, and the curve of an aeroplane's track
Meets the straight skyline.

The images of relief:
Hospital pyjamas, screens round a bed
A man with a bloody face
Sitting up in bed, conversing cheerfully
Through cut lips:
These will fail you some time.

One day you will find yourself alone
Accelerating down a blind
Alley, too late to stop
And know how light your death is,
How serious the survival of the others.
You will be scattered like wreckage;
The pieces, every one a different shape
Will painfully lodge in the hearts
Of everybody who loves you.

Evidence

Along the wandering strand the sea unloads glass balls
Jellyfish, broken shells, its tangle
Of nets, cork, bits of wood,

Coral. A crooked line paid out on sand.
Here's evidence; gather it all up.

Time on window-panes
Imposes a curved edge of dust,
Hides dirt under the refrigerator, invites
The mice inside to dodge
Behind the revealing stack of empty bottles.
In the refrigerator the ice is growing
Into odd shapes; outside
The house, the cracks are spreading
In the asphalt; they reach out, join
To weave some kind of message.

Age creates
People whose wrinkles betray
How they smiled, with scars
Of operations. They have white patches
Where the sun has not reached them:
The skin grows hard on their hands;
Some of them have false teeth.
The flick of their lashes, the flutter of their shirtfronts
Is evidence of life.

The Apparition

The circular white sun
Leapt overhead and grew
Red as a rose, darkening slowly blue.
And the crowd wept, shivering,
Standing there in the cold.

The sharp-eyed girl miraculously
Cured by a beggar passed the word along.
Water, she said, and they found a spring
Where all before was dry.
They filled the jars with the water.

All will be forgiven, good and evil together.
You are all my children. Come back
In mist or snow, here it will be warm.

And forget the perishing cold,
The savage light of day.

Every Friday at noon the same;
The trains were full of people in the evenings
Going north with gallons of sour water.

The Second Voyage

Odysseus rested on his oar and saw
The ruffled foreheads of the waves
Crocodiling and mincing past: he rammed
The oar between their jaws and looked down
In the simmering sea where scribbles of weed defined
Uncertain depth, and the slim fishes progressed
In fatal formation, and thought
                                        If there was a single
Streak of decency in these waves now, they'd be ridged
Pocked and dented with the battering they've had,
And we could name them as Adam named the beasts,
Saluting a new one with dismay, or a notorious one
With admiration; they'd notice us passing
And rejoice at our shipwreck, but these
Have less character than sheep and need more patience.

I know what I'll do he said;
I'll park my ship in the crook of a long pier
(And I'll take you with me he said to the oar)
I'll face the rising ground and walk away
From tidal waters, up riverbeds
Where herons parcel out the miles of stream,
Over gaps in the hills, through warm
Silent valleys, and when I meet a farmer
Bold enough to look me in the eye
With 'where are you off to with that long
Winnowing fan over your shoulder?'
There I will stand still
And I'll plant you for a gatepost or a hitching-post
And leave you as a tidemark. I can go back
And organize my house then.

But the profound
Unfenced valleys of the ocean still held him;
He had only the oar to make them keep their distance;
The sea was still frying under the ship's side.
He considered the water-lilies, and thought about fountains
Spraying as wide as willows in empty squares,
The sugarstick of water clattering into the kettle,
The flat lakes bisecting the rushes. He remembered spiders and frogs
Housekeeping at the roadside in brown trickles floored with mud,
Horsetroughs, the black canal, pale swans at dark.
His face grew damp with tears that tasted
Like his own sweat or the insults of the sea.

A Poem on Change

What wind agitates the dust
Inside the Etruscan tombs?
They made beds for man and wife; the servants
Were buried in the hallways.
They sealed the door up and left the dead alone.

The dust in your pocket lay still; I saw you
Reaching inside your skin for money,
Envied the warm notes, packed safe
Against your liver.

You stretched out for your glass,
Blind as an old man in a dead calm.

Now your face looks innocent
As the Atlantic stirred up in storm,
Rattling its plenty on the pebbles.
The wind roared through your house and swept it clean.

Ferryboat

Once at sea, everything is changed:
Even on the ferry, where
There's hardly time to check all the passports
Between the dark shore and the light,

You can buy tax-free whiskey and cigars
(Being officially nowhere)
And in theory get married
Without a priest, three miles from the land.

In theory you may also drown
Though any other kind of death is more likely.
Taking part in a national disaster
You'd earn extra sympathy for your relations.

To recall this possibility the tables and chairs
Are chained down for fear of levitation
And a death's-head in a lifejacket grins beside the bar
Teaching the adjustment of the slender tapes
That bind the buoyant soul to the sinking body,
In case you should find yourself gasping
In a flooded corridor or lost between cold waves.

Alive on sufferance, mortal before all,
Shipbuilders all believe in fate;
The moral of the ship is death.

Letter to Pearse Hutchinson

I saw the islands in a ring all round me
And the twilight sea travelling past
Uneasy still. Lightning over Mount Gabriel:
At such a distance no sound of thunder.
The mackerel just taken
Battered the floor, and at my elbow
The waves disputed with the engine.
Equally grey, the headlands
Crept round the rim of the sea.

Going anywhere fast is a trap:
This water music ransacked my mind
And started it growing again in a new perspective
And like the sea that burrows and soaks
In the swamps and crevices beneath
Made a circle out of good and ill.

So I accepted all the sufferings of the poor,
The old maid and the old whore
And the bull trying to remember
What it was made him courageous
As life goes to ground in one of its caves,
And I accepted the way love
Poured down a cul-de-sac
Is never seen again.

There was plenty of time while the sea-water
Nosed across the ruinous ocean floor
Inquiring for the ruinous door of the womb
And found the soul of Vercingetorix
Cramped in a jamjar
Who was starved to death in a dry cistern
In Rome, in 46 B.C.

Do not expect to feel so free on land.

Swineherd

'When all this is over', said the swineherd,
'I mean to retire, where
Nobody will have heard about my special skills
And conversation is mainly about the weather.

I intend to learn how to make coffee, at least as well
As the Portuguese lay-sister in the kitchen
And polish the brass fenders every day.
I want to lie awake at night
Listening to cream crawling to the top of the jug
And the water lying soft in the cistern.

I want to see an orchard where the trees grow in straight lines
And the yellow fox finds shelter between the navy-blue trunks,
Where it gets dark early in summer
And the apple-blossom is allowed to wither on the bough.'

Michael Foley

Recruiting Song

At times when the good jokes flow,
The laugh bursts, nothing is feeble.
Such gold and frankincense and myrrh,
I am a river to my people.

I'd chalk the walls with Foley Lives!
If they'd believe that it was meant.
Dozing before their televisions
No one comes to touch my garment.

O for them all to enlist with me
And to embark, one glorious regiment,
All bustle, baggage and trappings,
Our splendid pride without a dent!

Let us all go down together then.
With such magnificence we would rally,
Six hundred of us, stiff with purpose,
Thundering down the wrong valley.

Heil Hitler

The path of reason's very safe
As I was taught. But I remember best
When Hitler Coyle broke into school
And shit upon the teacher's desk.

They labelled him a filthy coward,
His low action worse than stealing.
Punishment was suitably severe
From fear of such contempt, such feeling.

I thought it funny, even brave,
But didn't say. I lack conviction,
Taught this timid reasonable touch,
Castrated early on by education.

So help me, hooligans and blackguards all,
Your huge hands itching for the kill.
I'll indicate what ballsed us up
And you can settle it, as you will.

From *Instead of a Rose*

III: Svengali after Closing Time

I gave you all my good books
So proud at so much truth bestowed.
How marvellous to take and teach and mould!
I waited till the progress showed.

You never really read them though
And finally the truth – they're boring.
I gave up then. That bright transistor
With its crude metallic roaring

Seemed your lot. So back to the lads
For mad gay drink, real chat and wit.
Except that drink was useless weight.
I think I dozed. The talk was shit.

And now, legs straddled wide for grip,
Two fingers jolting in my throat,
The ugly froth comes up at last,
The puke's congealing on my coat.

If I admit a purge, a fresh start,
Will you receive me back? You can,
I'm sure, put up with pride.
You have an opening for a man.

IV: The Terms

At times I've had an urge to say,
You've a decent home, for God's sake go.
This life on the roads is useless,
One-man audience to a one-man show.

Over twenty years in the business,
Joker, juggler, trick-cyclist, clown.
I can't learn anything else now,
You set 'em up, I'll knock 'em down.

For my favourite little turn
I display the foolish and the small,
Mention Italians with their ice-cream
And Hitler with his single ball.

And I give a new performance now
Instead of telling how it goes.
You're stuck with a joke for a love song,
A pee-the-bed instead of a rose.

VI: John Kelly's Daughter

We will arrive back far too soon
And laugh about the honeymoon
Hotels with full amenities
As boring as the scenery
The one attempt at living rough
Gone haywire in an epic huff.
But oh what does it matter
I shall wed John Kelly's daughter
    In the Spring.

And if I have to act my age
And curb my D. H. Lawrence rage
No outbursts at the petty hates
Like 'darling' said in front of mates,
If the urge to greatness passes
And I praise the middle classes
Well it's time to learn to flatter
When I wed John Kelly's daughter
    In the Spring.

And though we'll both be far too sane
To ever reach a higher plane
Arriving back the way we went
Still mostly prone to argument

Well, I quite like our narrow range.
I'm sure I don't want her to change.
Everything she knows I taught her,
O John Kelly's comely daughter!
    O the Spring!

The Fall of the Bedsitter King

When the riderless horse re-
turned with a bloody
saddle I knew no one gets
through. And here the tea
leaves block the sink, the tins are
running out. No go,
decomposing food, soft crash
of soot, a thunder
of plumbing in the walls. The
drums speak death, death to
the smarty pants. Last entry
reads, 'The twenty sev-
enth day. I have relinquished
hope. God grant me strength
to do what I must do.' I
shall mount the crumbling
sofa when the time comes and
face to the attic
window, scream (a teacher in
a temper) 'You're not
fooling me, you know, you're on-
ly fooling yourselves.'

O'Driscoll

O'Driscoll scuffed the autumn leaves
And sang as he walked along,
A meeting with The Poet
Being reason for a song.

He met him in a local pub
And stammering and pale,

He bought him soup and salad rolls
And a pint of Watney's ale

And 'O'Driscoll', then the poet said
That eventful Saturday,
'You have the touch, go right ahead,
But do it your own way'.

So O'Driscoll left the shady pub
His youthful head awhirl
But mindful of pride and vanity
He thought about his girl.

My love, my love, my love he would cry,
I'll sing your hair your eyes your lips
If you'll just nurse me through my tantrums
And guard my manuscripts.

And thereupon he fell in a dream
Of Bridget, his lovely bride,
But he saw, as he dreamt, a big cocksman
Appearing by her side

And he bore her away from O'Driscoll
Away with the greatest of ease
With a smirk and a laugh and a muttered joke
And a fling of his bright car keys.

Away, away, from O'Driscoll, away,
Away to a Rugby hop
And Bridget laughed and sang and danced
Till she thought that she would drop.

Come back, come back, O'Driscoll cried
But a pragmatist was she
'Oh catch yourself on, wee lad', she said,
'You'll squeeze no books out of me.'

Then O'Driscoll roared and shook himself
And out of his dream awoke
And the dance and the girl and Flash Harry
Were gone like a drifting smoke

But he heard high up in the air
A typer, typing away,
And never was typing so sad,
And never was typing so gay.

From *A la Recherche du Temps Perdu*

Before the old tube and covers went out
And before Continental boots came in
From weird assorted teams wild garbled shouts
As down the baldy pitch, on fire, insane,
Ran stunted, three foot, forty year old men.

Such conviction, such truth. Now never again.
'Quasimodo! Swing on your bell!' we cried,
Uncommitted, gay, the last hard men,
Proud but not proud, so scared of phoney pride,
Whose rotten jokes were really crucified.

*

I remember the sickening crunch
As evil impulse won the day
And I tramped on John D. Murray's lunch

Or else, the same primeval joy,
The pepper flung in the rice dessert
Of Craig, the fat 'free dinners' boy.

Autumn Leaves

The beginning of another year,
The snack bar filling day by day.
They have made love by the Black Sea
And hiked across the U.S.A.

And now with debates and politics
They prepare a winter campaign.
Like the villain in a rotten picture
I feel surrounded by dolts again.

This year, though, I am less amused.
It may not last, I may be wrong
But there's a final deadness in the air.
I think I have been here too long.

Still I chance my arm at science.
It's a living. I have time to spare
Time for gazing out the window
At the trees on College Garden Square,

And time to imagine falling leaves
Are from some rejected Ph.D.
And the trees line up for the graduation
Of a stern young scientist. Not me.

And it's all just a question of effort,
A belief in positive thinking.
You don't know when you're well off, son,
While you've got your health you've everything.

As my mother is always telling me
I could be languishing in hospitals.
Yes. Or strapped to a chair in East Europe,
With some mad major punching my genitals.

I Feel, These Days

I feel, these days, I'm quite a sage
To like the trees and bit of hedge
That bring to my bed-sitting room
The seasons' poignant fade or bloom,
And sage indeed to know what palls
And so avoid the worst pitfalls
Obsession with my face, my name,
A false success, a falser fame.
But, still, an idyll's not enough
I find I need the sterner stuff
Lust's lack of taste and envy's pang
And sometimes evil's thrilling tang,
The awful bitches and the dupes
In theatres and writers' groups.

For in the end I know no poise.
By surge and ebb alone are joys
Of progress won, at length. First fool
Then something more, the golden rule
To learn in love and life and verse.
God knows I could be doing worse,
My twenty-second summer flown
And never forced to booze alone.

Into the Breach

And always frontier days are past
Of gods we've always seen the last
    As always we're appalled
By new reports, new forms, new rules,
New posts designed to hold old fools.
    'A challenge' it is called

When each new torture's coming in.
Ah progress, in thy name what sin,
    What endless talk of gains,
For democratic man's not meant
To know that ninety nine per cent
    Were left without the brains.

And so the idle years are gone.
There's weeding out and pushing on.
    Farewell, fair dreams,
The gentle Chinese wine mystique
The God of Discourse Honeysweet
    Are done it seems.

We moan and doze, perchance to dream.
How grand the purging gestures seem
    As idle fancy runs
On midnight trains to New Orleans
And gorgeous golds and glowing greens
    Far from the guns.

Of course the answer's something more.
The plucky British knew the score.

They learned their style and poise
And English majors shot to bits
Would still abhor their screaming fits
'I'm sorry chaps, such noise.'

Oh such cute tricks the British learned
Like being wrong but unconcerned
And why not, pray?
Since so very few have answers
Take your chance among the chancers
Bluff your way

For neck and nerve are lively goads
And by the most bizarre of roads
We're often led to home.
That scrappy play you can't control.
Mark one speech 'Body', one speech 'Soul',
It's now a brilliant poem.

And stick it out among the clerks.
A mad indulgent anger works
But rarely.
Just ride the punches as they come
A secret God, a public bum,
Like slidin' Charlie.

And then in time perhaps the day
When we at last have learned to say
'I couldn't care less.'
Who'd want to thunder like a bore
Of nineteen frigging eighty four?
On through the mess!

I'm Scared . . .

I'm scared to go away, chérie.
I've been before
but with chaps. They are a help. They
appreciate irony,

when helpless there's helpless laughter
    at least. Your conduct is
satisfactory, yes – but never yet
    tested under stress.

Might it pop like a broken bulb?
    (where was Foley
when the light went out?) Ah how shall
    we manage at all?

Who'll love our twisted Papish hearts?
    Who'll be our friends
in the time to come? . . . And think of the
    letters we'll have to write!

Sois Sage . . .

Sois sage, o ma douleur . . . I don't
    hate the young any more.
Let them greet with satirical
    signs of the cross

and smirk of their 'impecunious state'.
    I won't hate them
any more. Love's the boyo to
    see them all straight,

so I muse, for I'm soft as an
    inside leg this year,
all due to woman's passive power!
    Entends, ma chère.

This song and soft clip clop is me.
    It's you I trot to
tired and tame, melodious with
    new found gallantry.

Frank Ormsby

Business as Usual

Daily we speak of going, more and more
    That futile phrase 'consider the position'.
Where we come from there's water in the veins;
    Small farms have sucked the sap of our ambition.

Our choice seems simple. Duty says protect
    The children. Flee a climate that is rife
With poisons. Take them where the futures shine
    And doorstep killing's less a way of life.

There's Weir – he gave away his paintings, books,
    Dogged reason till it yielded up decision,
Went off to join the pigmies, quite resigned
    To heat extremes and ritual circumcision.

He shames us all, who dither on the strand
    And shun the breakers. Liberation calls
For embarkations, eager voyagings;
    Our roots have roots and resolution palls.

Some day will find us moving, more decisive
    In limb than heart, still scared but on our way;
Not pioneers, but lurching out, like Foley,
    Who spoke of going till ashamed to stay.

Interim

Five years ago we knew such ecstasies
As who in half-dead countrysides find strong
The least life stirring;
We sang first lines and thought we had learned the song.

Six months of marriage sobered us. We found,
Not disenchantment, more a compromise
Charged with affection.
We settled to the limited surprise

That day-to-day insists on, brought to bear
A tact to manage by, a quiet light
That gave its own warmth,
And knew our walking grown to sudden flight

When least expected. O, I loved those years
Of unforced loving, when the urge to stray
Was lulled to sleeping,
And hearth and kitchen sink were nothing grey.

Now, once again, I notice carefree girls
In streets, on buses. Tied, I can't but see
Their untried promise,
All the lost futures catching up with me.

The nerve to be unfaithful is the lack
That curbs my yearnings. Soon again I'm sure,
And pleased to be,
Of trusting wife, my own furniture.

What binds us, love? I struggle to define
Its shifting substance. What strange seeds are met
Within us, fashion there in our despite
This hybrid, half-contentment, half-regret?

Tonight, uncertain if the dreams have cracked,
Let's seek behind the possible illusions
How much is gone, how much remains intact;
Let's talk of change and come to no conclusions.

Winter Offerings

Mother, it pains me that I must confide
To verse these clarities. We're each alone.
Our speech gutters. More than marriage divides
Us. Each visit home
I measure distances and find them grown.

It's your own fault, really. My good at heart
You grasped the chances that would sunder us.
I'm glad you chose to play the dogged part,

Take on the opposition. Often I wonder
How you prevailed against that blunderbuss

My father. What-was-good-enough-for-him –
The peasant's caution rather than a ploy
To keep me tethered; but you saw how grim
The prospects. Trapped yourself, you rescued me
From lives I guess at. Then, how could I joy

In love so functional, how call it love
That hid and whispered in a tough concern
With Grants and Benefits? So, schooled above
You, I grew up to miss those transferred yearnings.
School's out, but now in retrospect I learn.

Discarded woman, shame is turning me
To wish you mornings, and a folding night
Whose dreams are gentle, sight enough to see
This late guest bowed with winter offerings
Who turns his face into your going light.

In Great Victoria Street

The Belfast Pure Ice & Cold Storage Co. Ltd.

Your broad face gives nothing away,
Its red is neither blush nor blood-pressure.
The frigid is your way of life; your heart
Cannot afford to melt, and if it does,
Your blood is freezing water.

The sun can never make its mark on you,
Your element the frosty night, the thaw
Your enemy. I cannot burn with friendship,
Cannot light a candle for you, fire you
With love. Your plight is woeful.

Perhaps these lines may frown on your behalf,
A makeshift gargoyle, channel the release
You dare not. Or, better, borrow silence

From a gloom that words betray.
The great laments are dumb.

Floods

At high tide the sea is under the city,
A natural subversive. The Farset,
Forced underground, observes no curfew,
And, sleepless in their beds, the sullen drains
Move under manholes.

Blame fall on the builders, foolish men.
This strained civility of city, sea, breaks
Yearly, snapped by native rains,
Leaving in low streets the sandbagged doors,
The furnished pavements.

Dublin Honeymoon

For a whole week we walked the same beat,
Through Stephen's Green, whatever the weather,
Collecting travel stains on Grafton St.,
Past Trinity, O'Connell Bridge, the Quays.
Back at the hotel we bathed together,
Dispensing with the last formalities.

Our first time in Dublin. Not quite at home
But feigning ease, our moves were tentative.
As yet lacking the confidence to roam
Freely, we kept to our accustomed lap,
Were grateful for it.
Later we branched out and didn't need the map,

And laughed to remember. Without a wince
We've been exploring alleys ever since.

Hairy Horseworm

At sea between door and dresser,
Hairy-horseworm. On this kitchen floor
Your bristle with business. Ahead of you
My left boot menaces your guileless ripple.

The innocence of straight courses
Informs your sail. To learn from experience
Is not your concern. Instinct, your pilot,
Finds new bearings; trust is your crew;

I am colossus to your passing through.

Three Domestic Poems

1. SPOILT CHILD

The need to keep you smiling is my licence,
My chance to play. In our house decorum's
Had its day; immune to embarrassment
I prance and creep, speak Hottentot, wag thumbs,
And prod and tickle you; stand on my head
(Your mother can't do that), jabbing one knee,
Then the other. Sanity will seem dead
After this. Daughter, dear, you're spoiling me.

2. POEM FOR PAULA

I cock my fingers at the wall for you
And look, a rabbit! A poor specimen, granted,
Black and bodiless, but the best I can do,
And you accept it. See its ears! Slanted
Now, now wagging! For my next trick watch me pull,
From these crossed fingers, one black, flapping gull.

Timidly, in the tremor of first sight,
Your eyes experiment, tracing my arm's
Shadow till it meets mine. The helpful ray
Projects me mighty, worthy of your awe,
High priest, magician, primum mobile.

3. Second Childhood

So much for the safe period.
Ripe for company the sperm swam through,
The ovum kept a secret rendezvous.
Then: two inseparables, hand in glove –
Hey presto, love, you're full of life again.

Onan

What I straddled was cold earth. When I heaved
No eager woman heaved with me. The glad
Seed, pitched to its curious heights, burst. It was sad
That drying of spilt children. I was relieved.

The earth was indifferent. I might have cried
At the time; but the seed died, care ran
From me. I was my own man,
Wet with my own juices. Self-satisfied.

The Lord was not pleased. No matter then.
Flesh slackened, I was man alone
And less than I had been. I knew
Lives spent, the moment celibate,

The waste between relief and emptiness.

McQuade

When McQuade went up for a ball
He came down with snow on his heels,
And when McQuade took a shot the goalie
Had to hitch-hike back to the field;
A legend from the tall decades behind,
Like 'Bawler' Donnelly, and the Night of the Big Wind.

A quiet cancer stopped him, its tackle sly,
Decisive. Shocked, I watched him fall,
Saw Death collect him, easily as a loose ball.

A Brother

Being older, I was able for you then,
Won all the contests. You tried hard
And never quite gave in, potential Cain,

But less than lethal. Later I was still
Winning, had found in books a new
Arsenal and you, baffled, lost the will

To compete. We grew apart. The eleven plus,
The college years, drove a slow wedge,
Stretching what thin bonds were left between us.

Lately, when we meet, your talk defines
The ache of dead-ends, of roads not taken.
I note your hands are twice the size of mine.

Castlecoole

Foreign the planner's hand, the stone foreign,
From Portland drawn. Its journey the slow lurch
Of barge and bullock-cart, to Ballyshannon,
Then overland; a dour haul into our knowing.

You took to the soil here like a native,
But kept your strangeness. The ruts behind you,
Your last link with the sea, were only skin-deep.
They dried and left you here, complete in yourself.

A county circled warily about you,
But, hemmed in from the start, you did no damage,
Like others of your kind. Climbing your stairs now
I see you for what you are, a clean ornament;
I warm to your harmless symmetry.

An Uncle Remembered

You had no subtlety that I could see;
Thick words, livid with threat, hold

In the memory, your drunken sprees
Those months we roamed the farm, where – old,
Fat, bald – you reared pigs. Bachelor's joy, you sneered,
Regret for the girls you hadn't married.

You came to my wedding, uninvited. Guilty,
I found a seat for you, hoped you'd be civilized.
You ate your fill, cracked jokes about free
Booze, and made a speech that surprised everyone,
Generous, maudlin. We laughed at your awkward dress,
Your half-hearted passes at a fat waitress,

And laughed too, as the train drew out,
To hear your shout break through, half-sober,
Asking that the first boy be named for you.

Virgins

Supper was quiet. Apart as we'd ever been
We said grace, climbed the stairs
And entered that hour glad of proprieties.

No hurried spendings fathered debts on us
Our wedding night. Our peace passed understanding.
Tensions of two years found their release.

In that quiet room what marked our bed
Implied no loss, no slaughtered innocence –
Only a strain of waiting justified,

All small denials, hoardings of the best.
Love lacked a precedent, but found a way,
Surely as first kisses, hair on the chest.

Tom Mathews

Restless

my restless adulteress
pulls me by the elbow
if you know the way I ask
why do we hurry
we do not sit with the elders
at the city gate
we do not stand at corners
we hurry down alleyways
in the afternoons
seeking small darknesses
seeking cinemas for our unsocial love
in the evenings
we read the song of songs together
in the new translation
we read the companions' part in unison
reading sometimes to the close
sometimes finishing sooner
saying fuck Solomon
as an act of praise
her bed has a coverlet from egypt
her sheets are linen and sprinkled with myrrh
her husband has gone on a long journey
with a bag of silver
her nipples are brown as october
when I speak of future plans
she promises me winter will not come
drunk on dandelion wine
she promises eternal spring
in the mornings
my skin is ashen
we wake together
and drink alka seltzer laced with wormwood
in the mornings
my skin is ashen
my stomach eats itself
my ulcer is my stigma
I will not take it to a doctor

I need to feel pain
my restless adulteress
is ten years my senior
she is my mistress
she is my mother
pulling me by the elbow
showing me the way
she has come back from where I was going to
she is my teacher
she tells me answers I have no questions for
I am her pupil her foolish lad

The Singing Lady

We saw her in Linenhall Street
Behind the BBC
A small lady
In suit of sober tweed

And she was alone and singing
On that August sunday evening
When the light was failing
And her voice was high and trembling.

Just look at that
Said my female friend
What ever is it
Some sort of nut?

That is a singing lady I said
Singing in suit of tweed
With a tweed hat on her head
Singing psalm ninety-eight

Second version to the tune Stuttgart.
She is not nuts

She is a single lady transmitter
Her audience is her Creator
And those that pass her
Can you think of a better

Thing to do behind the BBC
In Linenhall Street
At nine-thirty
p.m. on an August sunday?

Anton the Elephant Boy

Anton lay on the circus floor
This was what they were waiting for
The great cow elephant Mary
Was on top of him nearly

And upon him she put
Her front right foot
There is nothing gentler
Said Anton there is no danger

The applause is not for me
Nor is it for Mary
She is only
Doing what comes naturally

It is to the glory of God
They applaud
For He made that great heavy beast
So gentle and precise.

Young Girl's Diary

A year today since I first
                was off with Michael
Met Des at ½7
Asked off with me
Went to our wee house
                under the bridge
It was great
1234!
I love Des
Des Des Des Des

He almost died when he was
            being born.

Met Dannie at the club
Asked off with me
Went behind the library
It was great
He was left-handed

But twice in one night
            isn't good for you

Robert Sat

The congregation were scandalized
When Robert sat in his pew and read a paperback

My mother said afterwards
'If he wasn't interested why did he come'

And I marvelled at her
For she never thought of applying that criterion to me

And I marvelled at Robert too
Able to read so calmly in the midst of so much hate

Robert is now doing very nicely thank you
He emigrated to Canada
And broke both legs in a skiing accident
And married a nurse

The Cowboy Film

When asked her opinion
The old lady said

The horses were wrong
You never saw a white horse

And the children's teeth were wrong
Children had rotten teeth in those days

And the women were very wrong

Another thing she said was the smell
But you cannot expect films to smell

Tom's Song

You should write a song Tom
Said my newfoundfriend
What kind of song I said
A song for today she said
A song about living
A song for real people
When she went home
I wrote this song

Is this a big lavatory said my nephew when he came to my flat. My nephew was three years old and well-travelled and he was right. I had not seen it before, the lavatorial look.

But I see it now. I see it in the blank walls, in the concrete stairs, the iron handrail with rust coming through the paint, the dust on the lightbulbs, the dried insectcorpses, the closed doors like engaged cubicles. The echo.

One evening returning from work I surprised a child peeing against the wall. A small figure leaning backwards, absurdly facing a blank wall, and a pool of liquid spilling over the floor.

I do not think I even paused, I know I did not scold. I think there should be a law to prevent architects building blocks of flats that look like lavatories.

I showed this song to my friend
She was not pleased
She said that is not a song
My newfoundfriend is too pretty to argue with
And I said
These days I am always singing
Let us file it under Popular: Male Vocal

Geriatric

I am not quite sure where I am
But I am quite happy
And I will write you a letter
When I find the time.

The Poet with Bad Teeth

Pale as death
and deathly loitering

We smell his breath
We hear him muttering

He is the poet with bad teeth
We are not listening.

Foolstop

for Joan

What stops me is the thought of leaving in a panic

L'Enfant Fatigue

It is nice to be tired Mother
And especially so when you know
  you need go no further.

Gustav the Great Explorer

He must have
Died or been eaten by a polar bear
The people said of Gustav
The great explorer.

Gustav had been gone
For a year and a day

He had gone alone
And it was a long way.

Across the snowy mountains
And the arctic wastes
That he was dead seemed certain
Now a year had passed.

But Gustav was not dead
As the people soon found out
When they saw him coming down their road,
And they all stood ready to shout.

It is not me they welcome
Said Gustav to himself
It is not me, but a phantom
Of themselves.

Thus strengthened
He acted out their fantasy
Spoke and dined
Like a true celebrity;

But unseen
He left his room before dawn
My life is not really mine
Unless I have my snowboots on.

NOTES ON CONTRIBUTORS

GEORGE BUCHANAN was born in Northern Ireland in 1904 and went to Queen's University, Belfast. He has written several novels, including *Rose Forbes* and *A Place to Live*. In London he did literary criticism for *The Times Literary Supplement* and drama criticism for the *News Chronicle*. During the war he served as an operations officer in R.A.F. Coastal Command and afterwards lived for many years in County Londonderry. He has published three volumes of poetry since 1958, the most recent, *Minute-Book of a City*, from Carcanet Press in 1972. He is now resident in London.

JOHN HEWITT was born in Belfast in 1907. From 1930 to 1957 he was on the staff of the Belfast Museum and Art Gallery. Between then and his recent retirement he was Art Director of the Herbert Art Gallery and Museum, Coventry. He began publishing poetry in the thirties, was central to the Ulster literary revival in the forties, and is very much part of the present flowering. He has published many volumes of poetry and appeared in many anthologies. His *Collected Poems* was published by MacGibbon & Kee in 1968.

PADRAIC FIACC was born in Belfast in 1924, lived in New York for several years and is now back in Belfast. He suffers from ill health, but publishes fairly regularly in Irish periodicals. His most recent collection, *Odour of Blood*, contains quite a few poems from earlier collections but is dominated by the horrors of the present violence.

PEARSE HUTCHINSON was born in Glasgow in 1927 of Irish parents and reared in Dublin from 1932. He learned Munster Irish from the Christian Brothers, and Castilian at University College, Dublin. Since then he has lived off his wits and his brains all over Europe. He is now Gregory Fellow of Poetry at the University of Leeds. He has published several volumes of poetry and some translations from the Spanish. *Watch the Morning Grow* was published by the Gallery Press in 1972.

JAMES SIMMONS was born in Londonderry in 1933. After a few years knocking round England he went to Leeds University and has been involved in teaching ever since. As well as poems and plays he has written many songs, some of which are available on the L.P. *City and Eastern*. He lectures in literature at the New University of Ulster. In 1968 he started *The Honest Ulsterman*, in which many young Irish poets first appeared. *The Long Summer Still to Come* was published by the Blackstaff Press in 1973.

MICHAEL HARTNETT was born in Limerick in 1941. He works for the Dublin Telephone Company, so far preferring this to teaching as a way for a poet to earn his bread. His work is much admired in Ireland and has appeared in numerous magazines there. The Dolmen Press brought out a collection in 1968 called *Anatomy of a Cliché*. He has translated from the Irish and adapted from the Chinese. The New Writers Press brought out his *Selected Poems* in 1970.

EILÉAN NÍ CHUILLEANÁIN was born in Cork in 1942. She was educated at University College, Cork, and at Oxford. She now lectures at Trinity College, Dublin. She has done a lot of good work organizing poetry readings in Dublin. One is surprised that she waited so long to bring out her first collection, *Acts and Monuments*, published by Gallery Books in 1972.

MICHAEL FOLEY was born in Londonderry in 1947. Like Seamus Deane and Seamus Heaney he was educated at St Columb's College, there. He took a degree in chemistry at Queen's University, Belfast, where he later taught Computer Science. He was an early contributor to *The Honest Ulsterman* which he later edited. His comic prose is much admired. He moved to London last year and teaches in a Catholic school there. He has published two pamphlets of verse, *Heil Hitler* (1969) and *The Acne and the Ecstasy* (1973) with Ulsterman Publications.

FRANK ORMSBY was born in 1947 in County Fermanagh, studied English at Queen's University where he later took an M.A. He now teaches English in a Belfast grammar school and edits *The Honest Ulsterman*. He has published widely in Irish magazines. Ulsterman Publications have brought out two pamphlets of his verse, *Ripe for Company* (1971) and *Business as Usual* (1973).

TOM MATHEWS was born in Londonderry in 1945, like Simmons he went to Foyle College, the local Protestant grammar school. Like Foley he went to Queen's University and studied chemistry. He works as a chemist in a cement works in Larne, County Antrim, where he claims to enjoy the routine. He has published two pamphlets with Ulsterman Publications, *Interior Din* (1969) and *Full Stop* (1973).